Dear Nicole
stay as sweet as
this book helps you to Know more
about the Arts.
Share your
thoughts with
me when ever
you can. I love
you very much
Nana
Oct 29, 1995 - 13 yrs old

Degas, the Ballet, and Me

By Tom van Beek

Illustrated by Thea Peters

Checkerboard Press
New York

This picture is on the poster that I gave Sandra for her birthday.

Monday, September 16th

I haven't written a word all day until now. And I almost missed dinner this evening. It's all because of a book I found in the library. Well, maybe it was really because of that poster I bought for Sandra's birthday last week. It was a big poster, of a group of ballet dancers.

Sandra loved it, especially since she studies ballet. She's been at it for ages, as long as I've known her. She is so slim and willowy that I'm jealous. Well, not really jealous, I suppose, because Sandra is my best friend. I can tell her anything and it won't go any further. I have even let her read my diary.

Sandra is really great, but sometimes she can be kind of spiteful. Like today in class. The bell rang and we all started talking and collecting our books and scraping chairs on the floor. I had just gotten my things together when someone knocked over my whole pile of books. Just as I was bending down, Sandra leapt forward to help, just as if she was at the ballet. She bent forward with such elegance and picked up all my books. She didn't even bend her knees.

"Here, Anne-Marie," she said. "Be careful you don't wear yourself out when you bend down." And away she went.

She teases me because I don't like sports much. I read a lot, and she has no time for reading

It was raining out and as I pulled on my raincoat and set off for home, I could see Sandra making great ballet leaps across the puddles.

On the way home I stopped at the library to take out a book. Had I only known what I would discover!

"Hi, Anne-Marie," called the librarian as I walked in. Lying in front of her was a huge book.

It was one of those art books with heavy, glossy paper. On the cover was a dancer like the one on Sandra's poster. EDGAR DEGAS' BALLET was the title of the book.

"Can I look at it?" I asked.

"Yes," she said, "but be careful."

I carried it to a table where I could sit and read. Then I just opened it, nowhere special. There in front of me was a picture of ballet dancers.

I closed my eyes and imagined myself once again at the ballet I went to last year. It was a performance in a real theater near Sandra's ballet school, and she was dancing. I just had to see it! It all came back to me; the buzz of the audience waiting for the curtain to rise, and then, with the slow dimming of the lights, the theater is quiet. Suddenly,

music—not rock music or anything like it, but classical music, very beautiful and exciting. It just draws you right in.

The curtain went up and the dancers came on. The ballet was *Swan Lake*, and it was just like the fairy tale. The stirring music, the patterns of the dance always changing, the wonderful stage settings, and the mysterious play of light, color, and shadow! The dancers turned and leapt off the ground as if they had no weight at all. The gorgeous white tulle of their whirling tutus looked like floating clouds. With every turn they made, the spangles and sequins on their costumes sparkled under the bright lights . . . it was wonderful!

Watching ballet made me feel as if I were in a magical place where everyone is feather-light and can leap with no effort. It looked so easy. How wonderful to be a ballet dancer and be able to make the audience feel as if they're in another world!

Suddenly I was back sitting in the library. Through Degas' drawing the whole world of ballet had come back to me. Who was this artist that could draw me so completely into the atmosphere of the ballet again?

Eager for more, I turned the pages. I looked at another drawing: the ballet is over and the dancers are taking their bows. One of the dancers has received a bouquet of flowers. She stands at the front of the stage and makes a curtsey. She is, of course, the main dancer. The *prima ballerina* is what you are called when you dance the main part.

The dancers in this drawing look as if they are just coming onstage.

Degas often made several drawings of the same scene, like these two.

Degas must have loved the ballet. How wonderfully he captured the ballet and the dancers on paper! He put thousands of little details into his sketches. I wonder if one of those two men talking in the wings is Degas?

I turned to the beginning of the book and read: "One of the most important subjects for Degas as an artist was the ballet. He made over fifteen hundred sketches, drawings, paintings, pastel drawings, and sculptures with the ballet as the subject. His paintings and his drawings were not just of the performances on the stage, but also show the ballet dancers in the wings, in their dressing rooms, during rehearsals, at fittings for their costumes, or resting from the strenuous work of ballet dancing . . ."

The strenuous work? It all seemed so light and airy, not just the real thing, but in Degas' drawings and paintings as well.

I turned more pages. There was a picture of a dancer tying her shoe.

Sandra says the only boring thing about being a ballet dancer is sewing ribbons on your shoes.

"It's six o'clock. We are closing now," I heard a voice say. I hadn't noticed that people had been passing me, one after the other, on their way out. I walked back to the checkout counter with the book.

"May I borrow this book?" I asked.

"No, I'm sorry—it is reserved for somebody. But I will take your name down and reserve it for you next. You can pick it up when it's returned. But you must get a move on, it's getting late!"

It was late indeed! When I got home, my family were all at the table, and they were already eating dessert. Dad was angry and said so. Mom looked grim and my brother David started pestering me, saying, "You've been to your friend's house, haven't you?"

Well, David wasn't far from the truth. I had discovered a new friend, and his name was Edgar Degas.

Sunday, September 22nd

Hooray! I don't have to wait for the Degas book from the library. I got it yesterday for my birthday, from Mom and Dad. Now I can look at it any time.

I talked about the Degas book all week. At first I thought they hadn't taken any notice, because there was a different book nicely wrapped for me at the

Degas in a photo taken in Dieppe, France, an artists' meeting place.

breakfast table. Well, it was a nice enough present, a nice enough book to read. I liked it, but I really wanted the Degas book.

Then in the afternoon when I had a small party, there it was, the real present! EDGAR DEGAS' BALLET. Of all the gifts I received from my family and friends, that was definitely the best.

After everyone left, I went to my room to look at my Degas book. All those pictures! I wish Sandra had stayed. We could have looked at the pictures together. But she wasn't really interested.

"You just look at it," she said when I suggested it, "and let me get on with my dancing." Then she left.

Anyway, I still think that Sandra and I really do understand one another. We both love ballet, but in our own different ways.

Wednesday, October 2nd

Sunday I had lunch at Sandra's. She has no dance lessons on Sundays, so we can do things together. Even so, she doesn't stop thinking about ballet.

Sandra knows exactly what she wants to be when she grows up: a ballet dancer. And she puts that before all else. You can tell by the way she walks, how she looks in the mirror, and how she listens to music. I wish I knew what I really wanted to do.

"Don't you ever find it's too much for you, all this ballet?" I asked her.

"What do you mean?"

"Well, all those exercises—it must be really tiring."

"No, I love it," said Sandra. "It's great."

"Do you really mean that?" I asked.

"Of course I mean it. You should try it out yourself some time."

"Yeah, right, me doing ballet. I'd much rather read about it." Sandra laughed. She's not interested in reading, but maybe that's because she concentrates so much on her ballet lessons.

This is one of my favorite pictures in the book, although it's not of the ballet.

Anyway, after school today I went with Sandra to her ballet class. I said that I just wanted to have a look. There was a lot of talking and jostling for space in the small dressing room, which smelled like sweat and unwashed clothes and soap.

"This is my friend Anne-Marie. We go to school together. She wants to take a look around," Sandra called above the noise. The racket suddenly stopped and everyone looked at me. I turned as red as a beet. "Do you have to point me out?" I muttered.

But Sandra went on as if she had not noticed. I wormed my way between the girls. I did not see any lovely tutus, just cotton tights, some without feet. Here and there I noticed rough-knitted, footless leg-warmers, and tightly fitting leotards in all sorts of colors. Some looked like bathing suits. I felt really out of place among all those skinny ballet kids. "This is the ballet classroom," she told me as we walked into the ballet studio.

The studio looked a little like a gym, and it smelled like one, too. No one was in it yet, so I was able to have a good look around. It reminded me of Degas'

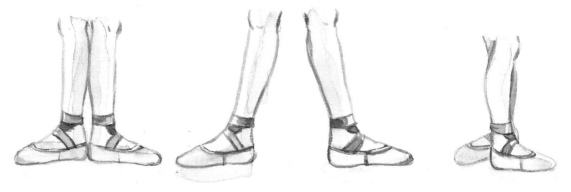

First position   *Second position*   *Third position*

14

sketches. I got the feeling that I already knew the place and that I had seen it all before. There was a wooden handrail running along the full length of one wall. On the opposite wall was a huge mirror. The floor was just bare wooden boards and on the other walls hung a few posters of ballet performances.

From a corner came the sound of someone playing a piano. The dancers started coming into the studio. They began at once to stretch their arms and legs, although there was no sign yet of any teacher. Sandra, too, was stretching diligently. Some boys were there, too—they came in through a different door.

Now, I thought, this is strange. In that whole Degas book, there is not a single boy to be seen dancing. Did boys dance back then? I had to find out.

Suddenly "At the barre!" was heard through the room. The teacher had come in. Everyone got a firm grip on the wooden handrail and was now facing the same direction.

"First position."

They turned their feet outwards. To be honest, it seemed pretty un-natural, the way their feet looked pointing sideways like that. But I re-membered seeing it in the Degas pic-tures of dancers at the barre.

From this position they moved their feet perfectly in unison, forward and backward in time to the piano. Then they swung their feet higher. Anyone who didn't get it right had to do it again and again, until it was perfect.

"En plié!"

Fourth position   *Fifth position*   *Plié*

Perhaps this lady is waiting for her friend at the ballet studio.

Next all arms went up as everyone bent their knees. Just watching them made me feel tired. What a lot of practice it takes so you can float across a stage as if you are weightless! Many exercises seemed more like torture to me than dancing.

I realized that what I was looking at was just what Degas had seen: the same movements, the same positions of the arms, the same turn of the feet. It was like sitting in some kind of time machine! The only things that had changed were the clothes.

"Warming up" went on for a full hour and a half. I would have given up long before that. They practiced over and over, just like Degas sketched over and over again. "That wasn't just to make our muscles supple," Sandra explained later, "but also to help us find our balance."

At last the teacher gathered all the dancers around her. She said, "You can do your best and you can do your very best. Your best comes when you have control of your muscles and when all your steps go right. But your very best comes when you have the feeling that you are really dancing and that each and every one of your movements is expressing something."

She swayed her arms, she made a turn, she bent her body and she jumped. And I saw the ballet as it was in my Degas book. Ballet: lovely, exciting, sparkling in its movement, and full of gracefulness and color.

Sandra was standing at the front of the class. She swayed her arms, she bent her body and tried to copy the teacher, but as she turned she lost her balance and fell. Now guess who turned as red as a beet?

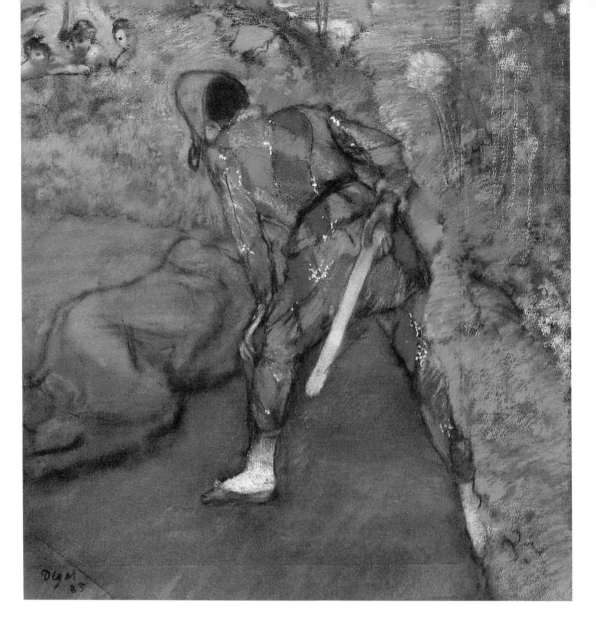

I finally found a man in my Degas book!

Friday, October 4th

I could barely wait for today. On Fridays we always have drawing lessons at school. We look at pictures by famous artists while the teacher tells us about the artists' lives, and he never bores us with dates. We talk about what we can see in the pictures; about beautiful drawings, paintings, and sculptures. I brought my Degas book to class.

"Well, today—"

"Could you tell us something about Degas, please, Mr. Paul?" I burst in.

"Why did Degas do so many paintings of the ballet? How did he get his dancers to seem so real? And why did he—"

"All right, all right! I'll tell you about Degas and his times."

"Great!" Sandra shouted.

So he began. "Degas was born in Paris in 1834 during the period of Romanticism. Who can tell me what Romanticism was?"

Someone called: "Being in love!" Everyone laughed.

"Yes, yes—but there is no need to laugh. To be in love was certainly part of Romanticism. After years of war and revolution the people had become great idealists. Everything beautiful made them feel good: love, the beauty of nature, stories from times long past in which the good always win. Whatever they created had to stand up to that ideal—the books they read, the paintings they studied, and the music they listened to. For us today it all seems very sentimental. But we have an art form in which everything comes together: a story, music, and spectacle. Who knows what it is?"

"Ballet," said Sandra.

"That's it. Ballet fit exactly with the ideals of the Romantic Period. That's when it really blossomed. Dance techniques became more and more refined until it began to look as if the dancers were floating across the stage. They became beautiful nymphs and fairies, or gorgeous princesses. It guaranteed success!

The man coming out the door in this photo is Edgar Degas.

My brother and I during the Romantic Period.

19

Here is a painting from Degas' romantic period. I prefer his ballet pictures.

"So, Edgar Degas grew up during the Romantic Period. He knew many of the painters who lived and worked in Paris. They came to his house, and his father, who was a banker, bought paintings from them. Those paintings were always painted from life and were very realistic. Everything was drawn with great precision with not one hair out of place. People didn't have to think about these paintings; they could simply admire them, saying, 'Oh, how well done they are!' Often the paintings told a story. They were mostly scenes from mythology or from the history of France.

"Degas started out by studying law; but he much preferred to draw and paint. Even as a child, and he always had art lessons.

"The Degas family was sophisticated and affluent, and his father was very proud of him. He was sure that his son had artistic talent, and he gave him lots of encouragement. Degas took lessons from Romantic painters like Monsieur Lamothe, who was himself a pupil of a painter you may have heard of: Ingres. Later, Degas went on to study at the art academy in Paris, l'Ecole des Beaux Arts. And you don't get accepted without good reason, believe me!

"Degas was soon able to paint as well as his teachers did. His paintings were realistic, like the one of his sister Thérèse, who was married to Count Edmond Morbilli.

"Degas' paintings were selected to be hung in the Paris Salon, the annual art exhibition. It was a great honor. He visited Italy where he had lots of relatives. First he stayed with his aunt, Baroness Bellilli, in Naples. Later on he went to Rome to study the old Italian masters. He tried painting in their style. Although that may seem silly to us, it was the usual thing to do back then—it was the way of learning the artist's craft. These studies had a great influence upon Degas' own way of working.

I think the photo and the portrait of Degas really look alike!

Degas   Cezanne   Monet   Renoir

"Around 1865 Degas returned home to France from his travels around Italy. He had become an accomplished painter, but he was tired of the kind of overdone, realistic painting that was popular at the time. He no longer wanted to paint by rules laid down by others. 'I want to paint in some other way,' he thought. 'In a way that no one has ever done.' He could think like this because he had enough money, and did not have to sell his paintings to survive.

"What he wanted was to bring an atmosphere to his pictures. He felt that there had to be life within a painting, so he began to interest himself in movement. He wanted to paint people in action, people actually involved in doing something. That is what he found in ballet and at the racetrack. Movement is difficult for a painter to express, yet that was the task Degas set himself, and he worked at it for the rest of his life. And how did he manage to provide this impression of movement?"

"Degas was an Impressionist!" called out Tobias, who always knew it all.

"No, he was not exactly an Impressionist," answered Mr. Paul.

"Why not?" asked Tobias boldly.

"Impressionists were interested in the play of light upon their subjects. Degas was more concerned with showing the movement of his subjects. But he certainly had much in common with the Impressionists, although he had in fact not heard of them at that time.

"Degas, like the Impressionists, wanted to be free of the studio. He wanted to be closer to his subjects. The Impressionists went out with their easels to find nature and light, but Degas took his sketch pad to the theater and the racetrack. What Degas wanted, just as the Impressionists did, was to paint in a different manner. A bit like . . ."

"Michelangelo!" someone said.

"Van Gogh!" Tobias called again.

But that was not difficult to guess because there were three Van Goghs, full of cheerful, bright color, on the classroom wall.

"Picasso," I said.

"So there you are: examples of artists, all of whom tried to do something different. Some did see success in their lifetime; some were long dead before they were recognized."

Degas sometimes made photographs of the dancers with notations about color that he referred to later in his studio.

"But didn't they ever sell any paintings?" I asked.

"Sometimes they did. This was of course no great problem for Degas. Whether people liked his work or not, he just kept on painting. He stood behind the stage, he went to the dressing rooms and rehearsal rooms, taking in everything he could see. He saw the dancers as strong and healthy, full of energy and natural grace, not like the fashionable ladies out of those dull sagas and legends that he had been taught to paint. His ballerinas just loved to dance—they showed their pleasure in their movements."

I looked at Sandra. She was giving the lesson her full attention, nodding her head occasionally.

"Dancers want to dance and that is why they put all their energy into it. That, for Degas, was the reality. No nice studio portraits for him. The real world of the ballet was what he portrayed. You know something about that, don't you, Sandra?"

Degas often divided his drawings into little squares. He would then copy each section in paint on canvas.

Once you get Sandra started with a question about ballet, there is no stopping her. She went on about training and rehearsals and posture and the endless repetition of steps.

"You put everything into dance to make it as beautiful as possible," continued Mr. Paul. "And that is what Degas did. He sketched the same thing over and over until he had it at his fingertips. Only then did he start on the painting, just as all of you would do by rehearsing for a performance or a play."

I thought that was a good comparison. I had not really thought of it that way before.

The bell rang! I would have been quite happy for the lesson to go on and on. Degas just totally filled me with curiosity.

I have written everything down so that I can read it later on.

Sunday, October 6th

Hurray! A whole day to myself. David is out playing sports, like he does most Sundays. He hangs around me all the time when he is home; he's easily bored on his own. I'm glad he's out today because I have to prepare my speech for class next Thursday. Each week someone has to stand up and give a talk. Now it's my turn. For my subject of course I chose Degas. I hope the others like it. My talk will go something like this:

A painter with a lady visitor in his studio.

"Mr. Paul has been telling us all about Degas. I have found that the more I read about Degas the more I begin to understand art, almost as if I had a new pair of eyes. I now understand why he did ten or more sketches of the same subject, and he was never satisfied with any painting that he did. He never felt that a painting was really finished, and so he always found it hard to part with it. Even when he had sold or given away one of his pieces, he would always try

Montmartre used to be an artists' neighborhood. Here's how it looks today.

later on to get it back. 'Just to make it a bit better!' he would say. Degas often took back a piece of his artwork and then the owner never saw it again!

"Degas' father died in 1874. As the eldest son he had to take over his father's bank and pay outstanding debts. Degas left others to run the bank, and he made sure all the debts were paid from the sales of his work. But after all the debts were cleared, he sold very little, even though right through his life he could have made a lot of money selling his art.

"For the second part of his life, Degas lived in a large house in Montmartre, a kind of artists' village on a hill on the outskirts of Paris. After his death hundreds of his works that had never been seen before were found in the house. There were sketches, pencil and pastel drawings, paintings, pieces of sculpture, etchings—something of everything.

"There was so much art because he had worked so long and hard. He lived for little else. Perhaps that is why he never married—he never had the time! Mary Cassatt, also a painter, knew Degas, but they were only friends.

"What else should I tell you? He would spend his mornings at the racetrack and in the afternoons and evenings he would stroll the streets or visit the theater to see what subjects were to be found in the life of the busy city.

"His craft was very important to him. He felt more at home with his painting supplies and sketch pads than he did with people. He was very independent, not only because he could afford to be, but also because he had his own firm ideas about everything. He always said exactly what he felt, but he hated to be criticized. He once did a painting for a friend, the artist Edouard

watercolor paper

assorted paper

paintbrushes

pencils

copper plate and etching needle

portfolio

turpentine

watercolors

pastels

ink and pens

palette

oil paints

palette knife

linseed oil

mixing dishes

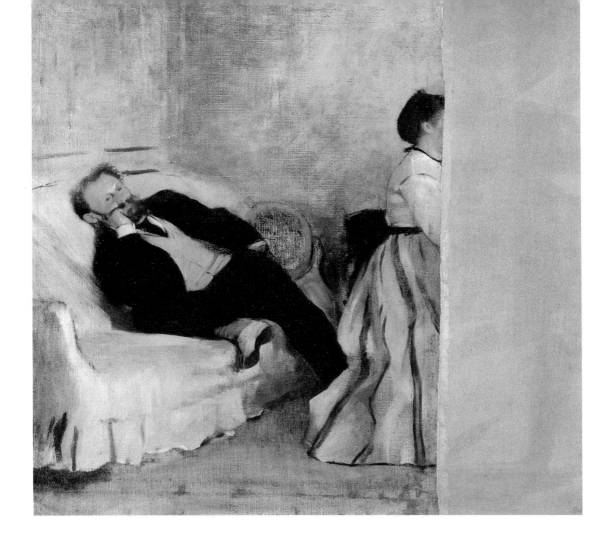

Manet. It was a double portrait of Manet and his wife. Degas painted Madame Manet dressed up as if she was going out, but Edouard felt that his wife was not beautiful enough in the painting, so he tore it in two and threw away the half on which she was portrayed. Degas did not find this funny. He never spoke another word to Manet. He must not have been the easiest person in the world to get along with.

"Degas was very independent in his choice of subjects. He never painted just what the public wanted. He only painted what he liked. He didn't care what people thought about his work.

"Of course Degas had a few friends with whom he could talk about his work. But they were usually not painters. He had a good friend, Monsieur Halévy, the author of a number of operettas, with whom he often went out. Monsieur Halévy took Degas to the theater and that was how Degas discovered the ballet. Degas also had some friends who were musicians.

Here I am from the front *from the top* *from the side* *from below*

"But it was the ballet that fascinated him. He could never have enough of it. He felt he would never be able to reproduce the ballet's atmosphere in his art. That's what made it so exciting and challenging, and why he returned, time and time again, to the dressing room, the rehearsal studios, and the theater. Over the years he attempted a variety of styles and techniques: pencil, chalk, charcoal, oil paint, pastel, and even etching and printing from copper plates.

"His early ballet paintings are very different from his later ones. That's natural enough. Degas could not, all at once, just drop everything he had learned before: that strong shape, that realistic likeness, that expression. That is why, at the beginning, his work is, well, how should I put it . . . more reserved than it was later on.

"He made sketches of the dancers during lessons, doing various exercises, just like the ones I saw the other day at Sandra's ballet class. In those sketches he tried to suggest the mood of the whole lesson. You can see how he was searching for balance, both the balance of the dancers and a balance within the pictures.

"As time went by, Degas tried more and more to capture the movement of the dance, not only in form, but also in color. That is why he tried different art techniques. There was, however, another reason. Degas was gradually losing his sight. What a terrible thing to happen to a painter! He was becoming unable to see shape and form. When he had to look hard at something, he saw orange dots, like you might see on a defective TV set. It became impossible for him to see what was going on.

"He began to notice it when he was in Louisiana, in America in 1872. He returned to France as soon as he could because he thought his problem was caused by the strong American light. But he had an eye disease which, in those days, was incurable. He knew he was going blind, so he began a race against time. That is why his lines became plainer and simpler. He began to use strong, deep colors. Atmosphere became more important than telling a story, but the story was never completely left out. He also started to sculpt small figures. To be able to see well was not as important in this form—he could feel his way. His first figure, "The Dancer of Fourteen," with a real skirt and hair ribbon, was first

shown at the Paris exhibition in 1881. It got bad reviews and it was the last time Degas showed any of his sculptures. He kept them to himself, and everyone was surprised to find them when his studio was cleaned up after his death.

"Because of his blindness, Degas almost stopped going out, but he kept

I don't know why they didn't like this sculpture!

working at his art at home. Sometimes dancers came and posed for him. But by 1908 he could no longer paint, and from then on he lived a very quiet life. He had few friends, and new friends were hard to come by. Later a niece came to live with him and to look after him. Meanwhile he was discovered by the general public.

Edgar Degas, old and blind

No artist since Degas has devoted so much of his art to the ballet. But you can still go to the ballet with Degas!"

His art was popular and fetched very good prices—in fact, more was paid for his work than for that of any other living artist at the time. Yet it gave Degas very little pleasure.

"Edgar Degas lived until he was 83. He was buried in the famous Paris cemetery, Père Lachaise, the resting place of many other great artists.

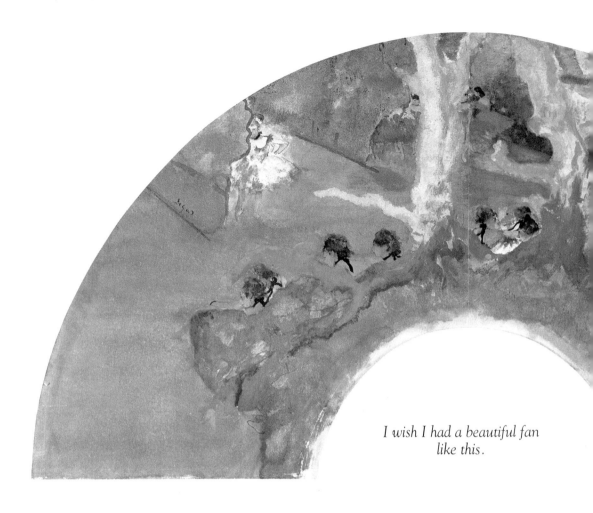

*I wish I had a beautiful fan
like this.*

Wednesday, October 9th

Sandra came to my house for dinner. We were sitting in my room with my Degas book between us, talking about the lesson we had last Friday.

"What did you think about Mr. Paul's talk on Degas?"

"It was good," said Sandra. "He really understands what ballet is like. You know, his talk has got me thinking about what dancing means to me."

"His talk about ballet, you mean?"

"Yes. We exercise and exercise a certain movement until we get it right. Then in the performance, all the exercising doesn't show. To the audience it just looks like the most natural thing in the world. They only see the dancing, not all the hard work behind it. Everything has to be perfect."

"No effort should ever seem to have beeen put into it," I answered. "That's what Degas said. He also said that nothing in art comes by chance. Just like

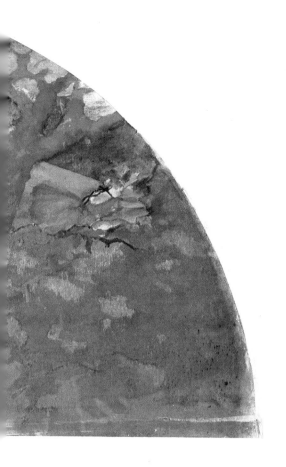

make him go away.

"That artist? He was just girl crazy. He spent his whole life staring at ballerinas." David started paging through the book. "Here! You can see him behind the stage, spying on all the dancers."

"What would you paint, if you were an artist?" Sandra asked.

"Well, certainly not dancers. Maybe sports or something."

"Like horse-racing?" I asked. I had an idea.

"Yeah. That kind of stuff," David answered.

I quickly flipped through the pages of the book until I found the pictures of jockeys seated on their mounts. Riding was another subject that Degas was fond of, and it's easy to see why. He was drawn to the movement, the gracefulness of the

what you have been saying—it takes tons of exercising to make something very difficult appear very easy."

"If you want to fix a movement in time . . ." Suddenly the door burst open and David was there, striking a silly pose.

"I'm fixing a movement!" he said, giggling.

"Mind your own business," replied Sandra. "You shouldn't be eavesdropping."

"We were talking about Degas and the ballet," I told him, hoping to

My brother posing.

riders, and the power of the horses. You could almost feel their muscles. I showed David. "What do you think of this?" I asked.

He turned the pages and looked at the pictures for a while. "That's pretty good," he said at last. Then he quietly left.

We saw no more of him until dinner time. That was a good thing, too, because I wanted to rehearse my oral report, with Sandra as my audience. Luckily, she thought it was fine. I'm glad. Even though I've learned a lot about Degas, I'm feeling a little nervous about speaking in front of the class tomorrow.

David is impressed with Degas, I think.

Friday, October 11th

Well, I am glad to write it's all over. My report went well yesterday. No comments or giggling. Everyone seemed interested.

We had another art lesson this morning. Mr. Paul told us about all kinds of drawing and painting techniques, using Degas as an example. Degas used many different techniques. He used many kinds of paint, sometimes making his own from coloring compounds and glue, or thinning oil paints with turpentine. Later on he worked a lot with pastels. "Pastel," Mr. Paul said, "is a kind of chalk that can be used for drawing on paper. The technique is very old, but Degas rediscovered it at a time when everyone was painting in oils. He smeared pastels layer over layer in order to get the cloudy effect of tulle and lace around his dancers."

I wanted to try this for myself, so I went to the art supply store.

"Could I have a box of pastels, please?" I asked.

"Dry or oil?" asked the man behind the counter.

"What's the difference?"

"Pastel is actually chalk, and . . ."

"Yes, I know that," I replied quickly. I was afraid he would think I was totally stupid.

Pastels come in so many beautiful colors!

My drawing, with David's "improvements."

"Well, there is oil pastel in which the chalk is held together by a type of oil, while the dry pastel has a glue binder. Oil pastels look greasier on paper."

"May I see some?" I asked.

"Yes. Here is a box of Rembrandt pastels."

"Do you have Degas pastels?"

The man began to laugh. "No, that's just a brand name, and it's a very good brand, too. It might be the same kind of pastels Degas used."

I bought myself a box with a long row of colors, and a sketch pad. It cost a lot, but I had to have it.

I went home and tried them out. It was so difficult! When I colored one area and tried another color over it, the first color disappeared completely. It all ended up smudgy and lumpy, instead of light and transparent. Degas must have had some other way of doing it.

"What are you doing?" David came into my room. He was bored again. He took a look at my experiments.

"That's not the way to do it. Let me have it." He grabbed one of the darker pastels and started to color hard over what I had done. Then he blended the colors together with his fingers. At first I was mad, but then I saw more life coming into my drawing. My brother was useful at last!

Well, it wasn't beautiful, but the colors were nicely blended. It struck me that Degas might have done something like that. When David left, I looked again at the paper. Suddenly I had an idea. I went into David's room and got his magnifying glass. He uses it for looking at stamps in his collection.

Back in my room I flipped through the pages of my Degas book. I was looking for a picture of a dancer in a pretty tutu. I found one and looked at a small part of it through the magnifying glass. I saw how the pastel colors

If you look at this drawing through a magnifier, you can see many layers of color.

were blended together.

The more I looked, the more I saw how clever it was. How did Degas get such rich and airy coloring with that stubborn chalk? I'll have to study his work long and carefully to learn his secret.

Monday, October 21st

I might be going overboard with my EDGAR DEGAS' BALLET book—I dreamed about Degas last night. He was making a wax statue of a dancer, and I was the model. He was wearing a long smock spotted with chalk and paint. He squinted at me.

"Stand on your left leg . . ."

I did exactly as he said.

"Now move your right leg to the back and look over your right shoulder at the sole of your foot."

It sounded a bit complicated, but I knew what he meant. I had seen a picture of that pose in my book. I stood, a little wobbly, but I hung on.

Degas set to work, humming a little tune from a ballet. It was a tune we had danced to in the theater. (Me, dancing! But in a dream anything can happen.) He was working away, with great concentration.

"I'm getting a cramp in my left leg, Monsieur Degas. Could I please sit down for a minute?" I asked.

"Yes, of course," he said kindly while he continued working.

I sat down and tried to remember the little tune he had just been humming to himself. But it wouldn't come back to me.

"How did it go, that tune you were humming?"

"Which tune?" he asked, without looking up from his work.

"You just hummed a little piece from a ballet. Could you please sing it again?"

I found these postcards at a flea market.

40

"Oh, that minuet! Of course." He took my hand, and then, humming the tune, helped me up and turned me around gallantly. It was sweet.

My dream then took a great leap through time. Degas' hair turned white and he became very old and completely blind. It was so sad. I felt really sorry for him. It's funny, but my age in the dream didn't change at all.

I dreamed I was a model in Degas' studio . . .

Sunday, November 3rd

Yesterday Sandra's ballet school gave their annual performance. I have seen very little of her in the past few weeks, because she's been rehearsing a lot. But I don't mind. Through Degas' ballet I have become much more conscious of the dancers' training, and the enormous amount of work that goes into each performance.

After the show there was a little party, and anyone who was in the show could bring a few people with them. Sandra brought me, and she introduced me to her ballet teacher, Madame Ponsardin, who had been a dancer in the opera ballet in Paris.

"You can still dance when you are older," she told me. She was full of the nicest stories; I could have listened to her forever. But she was a good listener, too, and she encouraged Sandra and me to tell her what we thought about ballet. Of course, the talk turned to Degas.

"Did you know there is a big Degas exhibition on in Paris now?"

"Oh, what would I give to see it!" I exclaimed from my heart.

"Couldn't we organize something?" asked Sandra, practical as always.

"Well, I was thinking about taking a few pupils with me to Paris during the school break," said Madame Ponsardin. "I want them to see a professional ballet studio and the training that goes on there. They could attend a performance, and maybe see the Degas exhibition."

Sandra looked at her eagerly. "Could my friend and I go?"

"Sandra, I was already going to ask you to come. You are certainly one of my best students. As for your friend here, well, I'll have to think about it. But if she does come, she will be able to tell us a lot about Degas and his art."

I can't believe it! I can go! Two months to wait and then: PARIS! And it's all because of Degas. Sandra's parents said she can go if she gets good grades on her report card. I'll have to work hard at helping her study over the next few weeks. Nothing must stand in the way of this trip!

Important dates in the life of Degas

Late 18th Century Degas' grandfather, a merchant banker, flees the French Revolution for Italy and later goes to America. He returns to Europe and sets up a banking firm in Naples. A part of the family stays behind in Louisiana.

1834 Degas is born on July 17th in the Rue St. George in Paris, near Montmartre. His parents name him Hilaire Germain Edgar. He is the first of five children.

1851 Degas begins law studies, but soon quits.

1852-1854 Degas takes lessons from the classical painter Lamothe, a pupil and disciple of Ingres.

1855 Degas is accepted at l'Ecole des Beaux Arts (Academy of Fine Arts) in Paris. This is an honor, but he does not stay long.

1856-1858 Degas goes to Italy: first to Naples to visit relatives, and later to Rome to study the old Italian masters.

1859-1860 Degas continues his lessons in Rome at the villa de Medici.

1865 Degas' work is shown at the Paris Salon, an important exhibition.

1865-1870 Degas begins making art about the racetrack and the ballet.

1872 Degas visits his relatives in Louisiana. Fearing approaching blindness, he hurries back to Paris and throws himself into his work. The character of his art changes: his lines become simpler, while the colors become livelier.

1874 Degas' father dies. As the eldest son he must attend to his father's banking business. He is obliged to sell some paintings in order to repay the bank's debts.

Edgar Degas

1875 Degas meets the painter Mary Cassatt, who is participating in the Impressionist exhibition. They remain friends.

1885 He spends more time drawing with pastels and experimenting with other techniques.

1890-1908 Degas is now old and blind. He receives the recognition of the art world and the public.

1908 Degas can no longer paint, but he makes up to seventy statuettes in plaster or wax of dancers and horses which will be cast in bronze after his death.

1914 Degas is "rediscovered" and his art begins to command high prices.

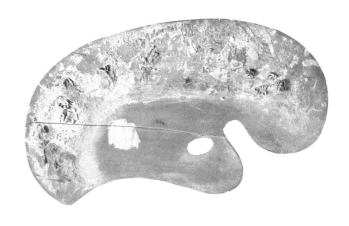

Degas' palette.

1917 Degas dies in Paris on September 26th.

Acknowledgments

Cover: *On Stage*, oil on canvas, c. 1877, Courtauld Institute Galleries, London, United Kingdom
Page 6: *The Green Dancers*, pastel and gouache, 1880, Thyssen-Bornemisza Collection, Madrid, Spain
Page 9: *Ballet Girls in White*, pastel, c. 1878, Private Collection
Page 10: *At the Theater*, pastel on paper, c. 1880, Private Collection; *Dancer with Bouquet*, pastel over monotype on paper, 1877-1878, Museum of Art, Rhode Island School of Design, Providence, RI, United States; *Portrait of Friends on the Stage*, pastel on beige paper, 1879, Musée d'Orsay, Paris, France
Page 11: *Dancer Adjusting Her Slipper*, pastel and black chalk on mounted buff paper, c. 1880-1885, Private Collection
Page 12: *Edgar Degas in Dieppe*, photo, 1885, Photo Barnes, Bibliothèque Nationale, Paris, France
Page 14: *Seated Bather Drying Herself*, pastel on paper, c. 1895, Collection of Bob Guccione and Kathy Keeton
Page 16: *Dance Foyer in the Paris Opera*, oil on canvas, 1872, Musée d'Orsay, Paris, France
Page 18: *Harlequin*, pastel on cream laid paper, 1885, The Art Institute of Chicago, Chicago, IL, United States
Page 19: *Degas Exiting a Public Restroom*, photo by Count Giuseppe Primoli, 1889, Bibliothèque Nationale, Paris, France
Page 20: *The Suffering of the City of Orléans*, oil on paper mounted on canvas, 1865, Musée d'Orsay, Paris, France
Page 21: *Self-Portrait in a Soft Hat*, oil on paper mounted on canvas, 1857-1858, Sterling and Francine Clark Art Institute, Williamstown, MA, United States; *The Young Degas*, photo, c. 1855-1860, Bibliothèque Nationale, Paris, France
Page 23: *Dancer* (also known as *Dancer Stretching Her Legs*), charcoal with white pastel, c. 1878-1879, Private Collection; *Dancers of the Corps de Ballet*, photographs, collodium plate, c. 1896, Bibliothèque Nationale, Paris, France
Page 24: *Dancer Adjusting Slipper*, graphite and white chalk on pink paper, 1873, Metropolitan Museum of Art, New York, NY, United States
Page 25: *Dancers in the Wings*, pastel and tempera on paper, c. 1878-1880, Norton Simon Art Foundation, Pasadena, CA, United States
Page 26: *Portrait of a Painter in His Studio*, oil on canvas, 1878, Galouste Gulbenkian Museum, Lisbon, Portugal
Page 29: *Mr. and Mrs. Edouard Manet*, oil on canvas, 1868-1869, Municipal Museum of Art, Kitakyushu, Japan
Pages 30-31: *Ballet at the Paris Opera*, pastel over monotype on cream paper, 1877, The Art Institute of Chicago, Chicago, IL, United States
Page 31: *Study of the Box in a Theater* (also known as *The Box*), pastel on paper, 1880, Private Collection
Page 32: *The Dancer of Fourteen*, bronze, cotton, satin ribbon, c. 1881, Paul Mellon, United States
Pages 32-33: *Three Studies of a Dancer in Fourth Position*, charcoal, pastel, and white chalk over graphite on buff laid paper, 1879-1880, The Art Institute of Chicago, Chicago, IL, United States; *Degas in Bartholomé's Garden*, photo, c. 1908, Bibliothèque Nationale, Paris, France
Pages 34-35: *Dancers and Stage Scenery*, gouache painted on silk fan with gold, c. 1879, E. W. Kornfeld, Berne, Switzerland
Page 36: *The Procession*, (also known as *Race Horses Before the Grandstand*), oil on paper mounted on canvas, 1866-1868, Musée d'Orsay, Paris, France
Page 39: *The Dancers*, pastel on paper, c. 1899, The Toledo Museum of Art, Toledo, OH, United States
Page 40: *Dancer Looking at the Sole of Her Right Foot*, bronze, c. 1892-1896, Marlborough Fine Art, London, United Kingdom
Page 43: *On the Stage*, pastel over monotype on cream laid paper, 1876-1877, The Art Institute of Chicago, Chicago, IL, United States
Page 44: *Ballet Dancer in Her Dressing Room*, gouache and pastel on cardboard, 1878-1879, Oskar Reinhart Collection, Winterthur, Switzerland
Page 46: *Edgar Degas in Dieppe*, photo (detail), 1885, Photo Barnes, Bibliothèque Nationale, Paris, France
Page 47: *Degas' Palette*; *Grand Arabesque*, bronze, 1892-1896, Musée d'Orsay, Paris, France

© Uitgeverij Ploegsma bv, in Amsterdam, The Netherlands, original title: *Ik houd van het ballet van Degas*.
Text copyright © 1993 Tom van Beek.
Illustrations copyright © 1993 Thea Peters.
English language edition © 1993 Checkerboard Press, Inc., 30 Vesey Street, New York, New York 10007.
Translated by John Tilleard.

ISBN: 1-56288-424-7
Library of Congress Catalog Card Number: 93-072400

Printed in Belgium
0 9 8 7 6 5 4 3 2 1